spiritual mentor in ways that are endearing and edifying. As she presents his view of silence, she shares her own meditative practice going deep into silence, becoming immersed in his images and metaphors, and seeking to understand their impact on her heart. She concludes her book with helpful suggested exercises that are about feeling, noticing and experiencing.

R. Melvin Keiser, Professor Emeritus of Religious and Interdisciplinary Studies, Guilford College, Greensboro, North Carolina. Author, with Rosemary Moore, of *Knowing the Mystery of Life Within: Selected Writings of Isaac Penington in Their Historical and Theological Context* (London: Quaker Books, 2005)

What people are saying about

Exploring Isaac Penington

Ruth Tod offers us a fascinating window onto the life and spirituality of Isaac Penington. She demonstrates that, despite the hundreds of years that separate us from him, Penington's writings remain a vital source of inspiration and challenge for Friends today. Like all good introductions, this book whets the appetite, and readers will be left wanting more.

Stuart Masters, Programme Coordinator (History and Theology) at Woodbrooke Quaker Study Centre. Author of *The Rule of Christ: Themes in the Theology of James Nayler* (Brill, 2021)

In this great new addition to the Quaker Quick series, Ruth Tod, lifelong Friend, is drawing our attention to the life and work of seventeenth-century Quaker Isaac Penington. She encourages us to look at his writings and thoughts meditatively and to draw them deeply into our own spiritual lives, now, in the twenty-first century. Ruth stresses how important it is for us to feel inspired and encouraged by Penington's beautiful words and ideas, and to see how they can enrich us now in practical as well as spiritual ways.

Joanna Godfrey Wood, Author of *In STEP with Quaker Testimony* and *In Search of Stillness*

In this book, Ruth provides an embodied and personal reading of the rich heritage of Isaac Penington's life and writings, It reaches out to those who know only a little, as well as to those who know a lot about his life and spirituality. Whilst it nourishes the mind, it also invites us to connect with the body as the source of learning and awareness. It offers to assist us, through carefully selected passages and practices, to find first-hand experience of the deep connection with the universal part of ourselves.

Lina Jordan, Psychotherapist, facilitator and Quaker

Ruth Tod offers us insights into Isaac Penington's experience, ideas and faith that springs from a deep sense of spiritual and emotional affinity with him. She paints a vivid portrait of a Friend who very early on, brought colour, warmth, heart and gentleness into the Quaker understanding of the divine, using poetic images that speak to us and uplift us to this day, more powerfully than any amount of formal theology. 'His words sing to me', Ruth tells us and she unpacks those words with empathy that makes them sing to us too.

Stevie Krayer, Poet and writer on Quaker topics

With remarkable clarity and profound insight, the writings of Isaac Penington continue to speak to us in our day, just as they did among the first generation of Friends. As a standout leader within British society and among Quakers, Penington wrote about his life-changing experiences with Christ, who like a powerful spiritual seed within bears fruit, producing other seeds and bountiful harvests of love, joy, peace, patience, kindness, and other fruits of the Spirit. In this accessible book, Ruth Tod brings readers into Penington's way of the heart, sure to bring forth yields of wisdom, peace, and love in the gardens of our lives, today.

Paul N. Anderson, Professor of Biblical and Quaker Studies, George Fox University

Isaac Penington is one of the most inspiring and thoughtful leaders in the beginnings of Quakerism in England. Ruth Tod engages him personally. While providing information about him, his circumstances, and the origins of the Religious Society of Friends, she shares the intertwining of her life with him as

Exploring Isaac Penington

Seventeenth-century Quaker mystic,
teacher and activist

Exploring Isaac Penington

Seventeenth-century Quaker mystic,
teacher and activist

Ruth Tod

CHRISTIAN ALTERNATIVE
BOOKS

Winchester, UK
Washington, USA

JOHN HUNT PUBLISHING

First published by Christian Alternative Books, 2023
Christian Alternative Books is an imprint of John Hunt Publishing Ltd.,
No. 3 East St., Alresford, Hampshire SO24 9EE, UK
office@jhpbooks.com
www.johnhuntpublishing.com
www.christian-alternative.com

For distributor details and how to order please visit the 'Ordering' section on our website.

Text copyright: Ruth Tod 2022

ISBN: 978 1 80341 184 2
978 1 80341 185 9 (ebook)
Library of Congress Control Number: 2022939087

A CIP catalogue record for this book is available from the British Library.

Design: Matthew Greenfield

UK: Printed and bound by CPI Group (UK) Ltd, Croydon, CR0 4YY
Printed in North America by CPI GPS partners

We operate a distinctive and ethical publishing philosophy in
all areas of our business, from our global network of authors to
production and worldwide distribution.

Contents

Also by the Author

Positive Parenting for a Peaceful World: a practical guide for the first twelve years.
Gaia Books 2005. ISBN 1-85675-236-4

Introduction

When I was a child living in Leeds, we used to go on trips to Airton Meeting House way out in Malhamdale in Yorkshire, in the north of England. This is a simple little Meeting House dating back to the seventeenth century, when people from the farms and villages used to gather on foot or horseback from miles around. Here my interest in early Quakers first began. I loved sitting quietly among the old benches, imagining bygone Quakers leaving their horses and wet coats in the stables before they came to sit down. I thought about their pleasure at being together at the beginning of the new week and what they had ministered about and endured for their faith. In the silence, there was usually plenty of time to reflect without interruption on their lives as well as on my own. I wondered how they had created a huge Quaker movement in just a few years. What were they saying that appealed to so many? What else was happening then? What had they discovered about themselves and their relationship with God, that gave them the confidence and conviction to spread their message in such an inspiring way? What can we learn from them now for life today?

Over the years, the Quaker way has been a thread through my life, shaping many of my perspectives and my decisions. I have appreciated the continuity and connection I feel with the early Friends; their wisdom and witness still nourish me. Among them, Isaac Penington who lived from 1616–1679 was one of the most prolific and poetic writers. From his own experience he shares deep truths with us and answers many of my questions. I see this short book as a bridge across the centuries, unearthing and opening up his discoveries, reminding us of their significance, connecting them to the present time. Much of what Penington writes, speaks directly to me, sending my thoughts in new directions. So this is about my journey as well as his. There are three parts. The first part is the background: my own background and connections with Penington, followed by the background to his life and the context in which his thinking developed. The second part looks at what Penington taught and believed using excerpts from his writings. The third part consists of my personal reflections on his work followed by exercises that can deepen our experience. My hope is that you too will discover the gifts that Penington offers us and find yet more wisdom, for the Quaker way is to keep learning and sharing.

The passages I refer to are taken from four sources: *A Month with Isaac Penington* by Beatrice Saxon Snell, *Quaker Faith and Practice*, *The Inward Journey of Isaac Penington*, ed. by Robert J Leach and *The Works of Isaac Penington*, online edition. (See bibliography).

Part I
Background

between our inner personal journey and outward witness.

I think this inner-outer connection lies at the heart of our Quaker way. At school I studied the seventeenth century and read Christopher Hill's *The World Turned Upside Down.* This was the period of the English Civil War when King Charles I was beheaded and new ideas caught on like wildfire. A radical new movement of Seekers was born, from which the 'Religious Society of Friends of the Truth' (Quakers) emerged. I was inspired by their actions and wondered what gave them their courage and confidence. I read T.S. Eliot's *Four Quartets,* and was drawn to his images of the still point of the turning world and time stopping as the last notes of the violin die away. I began to see the connection between stillness and movement. In quiet inward-turning pauses, we can find what we are called to do and be moved to act upon it. We don't need someone else to tell us because the deep truths about life lie within our hearts.

I saw that this profoundly new experience was the source of the early Quaker vision for the world. Out of the chaos of the war, the first Friends believed that everyone would soon become filled with the living spirit, making a new covenant with God and working together to build heaven on earth. The inward spirit was showing them the way. For a few years I was involved in Turning the Tide, a programme of Quaker Peace and Social Witness which offers training in nonviolent social change. We led sessions on the nature of power, including our own inner power that comes from self-knowledge and clarity. We also taught about the art of winning people over to create a movement. One of the basic principles of nonviolence is not *arming* ourselves against others, but *disarming* others with kindness, listening and respectfulness. In the case studies I read about, I saw the power of meetings for worship at shareholders' meetings and was moved by Martin Luther King kneeling in silent prayer before the troops at Selma. Here we can see what it means to call up our inner power to override temporal power, as the first Quakers had also done.

Later I trained as a teacher of the Alexander Technique, which helps people to move with more flexibility and flow. It is primarily used to relieve physical pain and break harmful habits, and in so doing the pupil becomes more aware of how they are moving and responding in different situations. Though the technique has no explicit spiritual dimension, I discovered a deep stillness that I had only paid lip service to before. This experience took me to a deeper place, to a connection with the life force within all. After a lifetime of pushing myself to do too much, I began to slow down and sense the power of stillness more deeply than I had ever imagined. I learnt to move with more ease and harmony, to soften my eyes in order to receive, to open my hands to listen to the rhythm of a client's body, as well as to my own. This kind of awareness comes from being still and calm, waiting without expectation, just noticing inner movement and offering support for what needs to happen for healing. I found another layer of meaning in the idea of experience, a new understanding of being aware of what is.

In Friends House in central London, I picked up a pamphlet called *A Month with Isaac Penington* by Beatrice Saxon Snell. Penington's words resonated with my own experience and clarified my beliefs about the wisdom found in stillness and the impetus to act out of that stillness. I copied out one of his letters and framed it. Later I prepared a meditation on it, which I shared with Friends in my Meeting. Now the letter hangs on the wall above my desk. We can see how his integrity and commitment came from continuing inward learning and a deep belief in people's potential. More than that, we can see how the embodied experience of a living God within gave him the courage and confidence to help create a new movement. He also reveals his vulnerability and compassion, offering his own struggles and learning as guidance and inspiration to others.

Now, as we face up to the huge inter-related challenges of

climate change, increased immigration, violence and distress, poverty and disease, more than ever we need to connect with our inner resources. In the stillness and waiting, I learn about the things we believe and fear. I stand at the gate between the world as it is now and the world of my dreams. My perspective widens and I see complexity and opportunity. Penington and the other early Quakers are asking us to see our world anew, to see the potential and step through that gate. The path is both an inward and an outward one, both personal and political.

have been times of chaos. King Charles I was beheaded in 1649 and eventually Cromwell, leader of the Puritans, became Lord Protector. Penington's father, Sir Isaac Penington, was a well-known Puritan, one-time Lord Mayor of London, owner of extensive estates, and was involved in the trial of the king and a member of Cromwell's government.

It was in this context that freedom of religious expression was witnessed as never before. Having shaken off the rituals and traditions of the Catholic Church, the Puritans replaced the altar with the pulpit as the most significant feature of the church. Teaching the Word of God in a language that people could understand was now more important than what many saw as the 'magic' of sacraments. With the arrival of the printing press, and the availability of the Bible in the vernacular, more and more people were able to read it and other religious texts for themselves. In the melting pot of religious and political arguments, the Ranters and Seekers were the strongest forces, asking questions and exploring new ideas on a scale never seen before. George Fox, one of the Quaker founders, brought many of them together when in 1652 he looked out over Pendle Hill, in Lancashire and declared there was a *great people to be gathered.* It is from here that we date the birth of the Quaker movement.

Quaker teaching crystallised what was already in the air. The Seekers believed, as did many others, in the imminent Second Coming of Christ when he would return so that everyone would be filled with his spirit and the hierarchy of the church would be unnecessary. Many pinned their hopes on Cromwell and his government to create a fairer society, as part of this new world. Fox and others, however, saw that Christ's spirit is already within us all now. This was not an intellectual idea but a total experience of the divine working through us and guiding us. Leaders, like George Fox and James Nayler were articulate preachers and writers who offered a vision of a new world, with everyone embracing a new covenant with

God and transforming society. Since there is that of God in each person, everyone would be treated equally. There would be no social or economic inequality and no need for church or secular authorities because everyone would be following God's guidance. It was all happening now, not in the future, but now, in the present. In these exciting times, the movement broadened, joined by many of the Levellers and Diggers who shared their political views. By 1660 the number of Quakers in England had grown to between 30,000 and 50,000 in a total population of just three and a half million and they were a force to be reckoned with.

However, this was the peak; in 1660, the Protectorate collapsed, the monarchy was restored and everything changed. Unsurprisingly, the Church of England was re-established and everyone by law was now required to attend every Sunday. Many Quakers were ex-soldiers who were now becoming pacifists so that Fox was able to say to the King 'we live in that life and power, which takes away the occasion of all wars'. But the new Royalist parliament was not convinced and turned on all dissenters, including Quakers, with a vengeance.

During this time, Quakers stood out as one of the earliest faith-based non-violent movements in Britain, integrating their religious and political beliefs, wherever they could. The difference between the personal and political was blurred. Each decision arose from deep inner guidance and prayer, in tune with the leadings of love and wisdom that they found in the silence. Their conviction was their rock and their compass. They refused to go to church because they believed that paid ministers, sermons, set prayers and accepted teachings did not engage people very deeply; what mattered more was the spiritual experience of all: children, women and men. They refused to pay tithes to the Church, which was an obligatory ten per cent tax. They referred to everyone in the social hierarchy in the familiar 'thee' and 'thou', rather than 'you'. Women and men were held in equal respect, both socially and spiritually, so within the Society of Friends, women's voices were heard and acted upon. All these acts of witness were a challenge to the status quo of society. The usual punishments were either fines or imprisonment for a few weeks or longer. So it was that Quakers established Meeting for Sufferings to pray for and support all who suffered for their faith.

The punishments exacted by the new government took its toll and the early evangelising energy began to fade. Quakers became more inward facing, accepting that the world was not going to be transformed overnight. The idea that each person makes their own individual choices based on their personal leadings, was now balanced by the idea of discernment within the community. In the Meeting, Friends reflected and searched together, so that a shared understanding emerged, where differences could lead to growth and further awakening. Their way of being together became enshrined in what became known as Gospel Order, which provided the structure that enabled them to survive as a distinct, less threatening church. Many Friends emigrated to America to colonies where they were free to practise their faith as they wished. In Britain, Quakers refused military and civic roles in protest against the status quo and continued their witness within their own communities.

Living Hope

I think those very early Quakers have something important to teach us about integrity, faith and hope. They trusted in their experience of the inner spirit of Christ, that gave them authority or power to speak out and stand up for their beliefs in every aspect of their lives. They had a physical as well as a spiritual and intellectual sense of what they were called to do, and this gave them their energy and confidence. Heaven on earth was literally possible, in the present time.

Today, it seems to me that many of us no longer share their

faith and confidence. The pioneering enthusiasm seems remote to most of us. Very few of us are willing to go to prison and suffer as they did, and as we have seen, their passion was not, in the end, sustainable. Most of us now have a more nuanced approach to life. It is hard to trust in a divine plan. Change is complex. Certainty has limitations. Diversity of experience and knowledge shows us there are many paths and many views. Unlike the early Quakers, we appreciate the importance of beauty and creativity; simplicity does not mean banning music and theatre, for example. We still hold the same core vision and values and we know that life needs to be lived now, in the present, according to those values as far as we are able. I am not sure that this is enough. When I delve into the writings of Penington and his contemporaries, I discover further layers of wisdom. What, I wonder, can those early Quakers teach us about the spiritual engagement that drove them?

It was from Margaret Fell, who was one of the vital driving forces of the early Quaker movement, that I heard the phrase *living hope,* which I think is a way of saying that *hope needs to be lived.* It is not simply a wish for the future; it is for manifesting now. Hope, in the strong meaning of the word, gives us a way to acknowledge what is happening and to face it with purpose and energy. Hopeful energy awakens us to possibilities, draws others towards us and encourages us to participate, through prayer or action, to make peace with ourselves and the planet. The early Quakers believed that there was a divine plan for humankind and now today, many people have a similar view, that we are waking up to a new way of being and that all is evolving as it is meant to. I look one way and see total disaster. Then I look the other way and see human beings finally learning about connection and equality. I do not know what will happen, but I do know that living hopefully is the best thing I can do. I also know that if we are ever to move mountains and transform society, our witness must flow from the love and spiritual clarity that we find in the stillness. We need to believe, as fully as we can, in the possibility of renewal.

Penington's own vision was of a garden, in which the seeds within us flower to create a garden that is walked in and watered by the spirit. Hope lies in our capacity to connect with that life within, and then to nurture it so that all will flourish. In the course of this book, I aim to explore the source of Penington's hope and what he teaches about the life of the spirit.

Mary and Isaac Penington

Penington is often described as a mystic, though he was also an activist. It is this combination of deep reflection and witness that attracts me to him, as well as the beauty of his writing.

As a young man, Isaac was part of fashionable London society and during that time, met and married Lady Mary Springett (née Proude). Both Mary and Isaac were Seekers. Mary's first husband, Sir William Springett, fought under Cromwell and died of a fever while serving. In Isaac she found a fellow seeker, whom she admired deeply for his beliefs. They began to read Quaker literature and in 1658 they became convinced Quakers. Penington started to preach and write and to stand against the Church.

I don't know how Isaac would have coped without Mary. Like many other Quaker women of the time, she played an important spiritual and practical role, which was gradually forgotten. She took charge of the finances as well as running the household and caring for the family. Isaac's family home in Chalfont Grange (Buckinghamshire, UK) was confiscated by King Charles II because of Penington senior's role in the trial of King Charles I. Mary had her own estates to draw upon, as well as excellent management abilities. She redesigned and supervised the renovation of Woodside, a much smaller house in Old Amersham, close enough to Chalfont to stay in touch with the Quaker community there. Here they offered hospitality and support to many Friends including William Penn, who married Gulielma, Mary's daughter by her first husband. In 1722, forty years after her death, some of Mary's written reflections were discovered and published in a collection titled *Quakers, medicine and property*. They reveal both her spiritual search and her practical ability to manage whatever life dealt her.

Altogether, Penington went to prison in Aylesbury and Reading six times, for periods ranging from a few weeks to a few months. Prison in the seventeenth century was very hard, cold, uncomfortable and cruel, only made bearable by the ministrations of friends who were allowed to visit with food, clean clothes, books and writing materials. Many prisoners became ill, and some died from disease and lack of care. Penington's early imprisonments were just for a few weeks, once for refusing to call the Earl of Bridgewater 'My Lord', another for walking in a Quaker funeral procession. During these times, he was able to write and support fellow inmates. His pamphlets and letters are full of advice and encouragement to Meetings and individuals. In a postscript to a letter written from prison in 1667, he says to his family:

> watch over them [his children] ... take heed of upbraiding them, or aggravating anything lest they be hardened thereby, and the bad raised up and strengthened in them.... Watch over your hearts and ways that ye may be examples to them.

Penington suffered no further imprisonments and died peacefully near Canterbury in 1679.

Part II

What Penington Taught and Believed

Penington wrote extensively and so it is possible to learn a lot about his beliefs and teaching. Some of the pieces, that I have selected, come from correspondence that he was having with particular Friends. The remainder are from pamphlets that he wrote to clergy and others in order to explain and publicise his views. The letters are written in a relatively informal way, while the pamphlets reflect the arguments of the day and are very formal. There are plenty of online resources for those who would like to read more.

As we read what Penington says, it is important to remember that in the middle of the seventeenth century most British people were Christian, many avidly reading and arguing over the meaning of the Bible and various religious tracts. Being a man of his time, Penington often refers to God as 'Father' and 'Lord' but also as 'the fountain of life', 'the light within' and 'the living seed'. Today in a multi-cultural society, many people find that words such as 'Father', 'God' and 'worship' are confusing, and some prefer not to use them at all. I hope you will be open to what he is saying, without judging him by your own assumptions. Quakers acknowledge that words are a guide to understanding, not ends in themselves. In the silence of communal contemplation, we can sense the connection to each other through the life-giving, loving power and presence that is everywhere. As we open ourselves in this way, we may awaken to a new way of being. I hope you will be willing to look beneath the labels and connect with your experience and the learning that Penington offers.

My aim here is to share and comment on some of Penington's writings from my personal perspective. His writings are so rich that, as is the way of Quakers, you may well interpret them differently.

Chapter 3

Experience

Finding Quakers

Penington's first Meeting for Worship was a huge turning point in his life. For many years he had been searching for God through reading and discussions and then in the silence he had an experience of the divine that he had been longing for. All his inner turmoil melted away and he felt renewed. He saw that God is within us in the stillness, where everything begins. This was a call to heal himself and create a new world, led by the spirit. He gave up the social life of a wealthy Londoner and embraced the 'homespun' simplicity of Quakers in Buckinghamshire.

Of his first encounter with a Quaker Meeting he said:

> When I came [to Meeting] I felt a presence and power of the most high among them, and words of truth from the Spirit of Truth reaching to my heart and conscience, opening my state as in the presence of the Lord.

He wrote at length about that experience, how he had *met with the inner seed, with God, with the true knowledge that is life, with the true peace and rest of the soul.* This experience would be his anchor and guide. His whole life would be shaped by it and he would give himself up to it, wherever he was led by the spirit.

Before he discovered Meeting for Worship, his life had been a struggle and at times a torment. As a child he had known a life-giving spirit, which he had lost and longed to find again. At times, he said, he went through dark times, searching for God, looking for what he had lost, feeling that God had forsaken him. Now he realised that God was not to be found in reasoning and argument but within us all. He sums up the difference here:

There is a faith which is of man's self and a faith which is the gift of God.

The first kind comes from the letter and is shallow, *like a great tree which is very confident and much pleased, not perceiving the defect in the roots.* Reasoning and argument, he says, are bound up with the ego, what he calls *fleshly reasoning and pride.* The other kind of faith, the *true faith is a gift of God.* It comes from *the spirit and the pearl within.* This pearl or *treasure* gives us *everlasting fullness and freedom from misery.* After all those years of feeling a failure, cut off from God and alone, he now felt healed and loved. He asks *dost thou feel the life and power flowing in upon thee from the free fountain? Is the load really taken off thy back?*

His words sing to me. Compared with the dry texts of the period, his writing speaks directly to us in phrases and images. *Rest for the soul* and *the free-flowing fountain* are powerful because we can see them in our mind's eye and also feel them in our bodies. As I read, I feel his passion and his vulnerability. When he writes about his search for the living God and his utter distress at failing to find what he longed for, I feel deeply sad for him. When he finds God in Meeting, his outpourings of love and excitement are very moving.

Penington has gone deeper than reasoning and evaluation, beyond argument to the place of spiritual unity. His use of images as metaphors helps us to feel our way into concepts that we only partly understand, to a place beyond words. In many churches, worshippers use specific objects for that purpose. In the Quaker stillness, we can create our own images and let our imagination wander through them. I sit with them, giving them space to speak to me. I may be drawn right into an image and feel it within me or I may watch it grow into something else. I muse

on it and sometimes find new insights or avenues to explore. As
I read Penington, I find myself contemplating the images that he
uses, in a Quakerly version of Lectio Divina, a monastic practice,
now quite widely used to explore passages in a reflective manner.
I read a passage and wait to see what happens. This is how I came
to choose the pieces here in this booklet.

God as Source and Presence

We each understand God in our own way, depending on what
we learn and experience in our lives. For Penington, the word
'God' is the source of all that is and the core of our being. God
is a name for the life that creates and flows through and within
everything, both a presence and a power beyond and within
each of us. In an essay entitled Questions and Answers he wrote:

> God is the fountain of beings and natures, the inward
> substance of all that appears.

To Thomas Walmsey he wrote:

> God is love, and he gives love, and teaches love.

The fountain is a powerful and beautiful image of the presence
of God as the life force. It speaks to me of being washed and
replenished, of receiving and letting go, of being part of a
universal flow. This energy is vast, both beyond and within us,
connecting us to all that is. It is within every person, a force that
is creative, nourishing, generous and supportive, that calls us to
open up, change and let go. It is an unconditional universal love
that touches our souls.

At the same time, Penington sees God as a presence,
accompanying him and teaching him. As a man of his time,
he often describes this as 'Father' or 'Lord', names which are
difficult for many of us today because they are often associated

with paternalism and patriarchy. However, it is possible to interpret the relationship of the parent and child in other ways. It may be that we are able to feel the warmth and support of unconditional love flowing from a presence that is always with us, accompanying and supporting us. Or we may sense it as our wise inner self, or as a universal, higher presence. The Quaker phrase *that of God within each of us,* may encompass all these meanings.

In this letter to Bridgit Atley, I think Penington is describing this unconditional love that is given to us:

> If thine heart comes to feel the seed of God... he will tender thee as a child, and his love will naturally break forth towards thee.... My heart is refreshed for thy sake, rejoicing in the Lord's goodness towards thee.

I think that behind those words, is something important about a relationship with deep wisdom. God is the wisest voice amongst my other voices, waiting to be heard above the inner critic and the inner child. It is a life-giving, supportive part of me that is also wiser than me, because it is beyond as well as within me, deepening and widening my perspective. God is divine presence that holds me. Whether this is real or a human creation may not matter because what does matter is our experience. For early Quakers, God was a lived experience that enhanced their lives and gave them an inner authority, integrity and purpose.

In the passages above and below Penington refers to the image of the seed, as indeed he does frequently. It is an image he keeps returning to.

> For grace is a spiritual, inward thing, a holy seed and is sown by God and springs up in the heart.

For me, the seed of God is a beautiful way of saying that we have all been given the potential to be wonderful human beings, to grow our lives so they are like an abundant garden. The seed is that wise and loving part of us which heals and teaches us. It is the divine within that can guide us. It is also our link with the wider divine, which can hold and support us. It grows within us and reaches out to all of life. The dance of life calls me to live with the sensitivity, generosity and fullness that I see in nature. I know that life is precious and wonderful, for living and loving now in the present. It is a calling from within. When I stop to listen, this presence can be a guide that challenges and supports me; it can open my eyes to new insights and help me discern where to go and what to do.

Waiting, Worship and Prayer

In his letters, Penington explains how we develop this relationship with the spirit through worship, prayer and waiting. Worship is another of those words that many people struggle with and again it all depends on what we mean by it. Quakers do not come to bow down; we come to be in the presence of this universal energy, divine love, deep peace, to receive and to learn. In Meeting for Worship, we create a safe space to open ourselves to this energy. As we come into the meeting house we might shake hands, take off our coats and metaphorically step over a threshold into that special place. We sit together and wait in the circle.

In a pamphlet called 'The Inward Path' Penington has this to say about worshiping together:

And this is the manner of their worship. They are to wait on the Lord to meet in the silence of the flesh and watch for stirrings of his life and the breakings forth of his power amongst them....

Our worship is a deep exercise of our spirits before the Lord... We wait to hear with the new ear, what God shall please to speak inwardly in our own hearts.

Friends describe the palpable sense of unity as a gathered meeting. Often, for me, this means that I feel embraced by compassion and generosity at a deep level, which I rarely find on my own. I feel safe to let love and light do their healing. Sometimes ministry is just what we need to hear, and our sense of unity is affirmed. I am sure that the early Quakers found in communal worship the courage and inspiration to witness as they did.

Silent worship, wherever it is practised, is unique because of the element of waiting. Into the empty space we bring our whole self. The intention is to learn and grow. It is to acknowledge and accept all our feelings and thoughts and to seek peace with ourselves through understanding. It is to see our lives anew and to be led where we are called, though as Penington says, elsewhere this may or may not be to great things. It is a step into uncertainty because we don't know what we will find.

I think Penington saw worship and waiting as open-ended prayer, not asking God to give us what we want, but opening ourselves to what we are called by love to know and do. Prayer is intentional. It may be a desire or request for guidance or support, a question or a conversation, a way to express thankfulness and a space to simply say 'here I am'. At its core, prayer is a time for opening our hearts and listening.

In the few references to prayer that I have found in his writings, Penington connects prayer with breath.

He says to a parent who is concerned about her or his children that prayer will come naturally when they find inward unity with the spirit:

As for praying, they will not need to be taught that outwardly; but if true sense be kindled in them, though ever so young, from that sense will arise breathings to Him...

In one of his pamphlets, he writes:

> Prayer is the breath of the living child to the Father of Life.
> Prayer is letting go of our own will, wholly out of our power
> – in the spirit of the Father who is the fountain of life.

In a letter from Aylesbury Prison to Friends in the Chalfonts, he reminds us that through our breath we are connected to the whole of life within and beyond us:

> O that you might feel the breath of life, that life which first quickened in you, and which still quickeneth!

Breath gives us life spiritually as well as literally. Placing breath and prayer together reminds us that prayer is a life-giving thread of connection to all that is. It is a way of being, just as breathing is. It is the promptings of love and truth, flowing from our hearts as we breathe. Attending to our breath helps us to make and feel those connections. Let your breath flow through your whole being, listen to it and allow it to guide and support you always. Let it lead you where you need to go and what you need to learn. Trust in what you find. I watch my breath flowing through me, moving up and down in the centre, in and out, over and over, gently, effortlessly touching every cell of my being. Reaching out to all of life. Part of a living network of flowing energy. Just noticing. Body, mind and spirit in unity. I settle into worship and wait. Penington reminds us to give up our own desires and open to what love asks of us, so that we can use our gifts for the good of all.

In order to experience the inward life, we need to be fully present with ourselves, open to receive and to learn. For Penington this was a practice that involved body, mind and spirit. Whether in worship or in quiet pauses during the day, we start by coming home to ourselves, just as we are. Some people may do this spontaneously or naturally, whilst others find they need help. As he went around the country ministering and nourishing new groups, it is not surprising that people asked Penington for guidance.

Over and over again, he encourages us to wait and all will be revealed in the waiting. Here he writes:

> There is a river, a sweet, still flowing river, the streams whereof will gladden thy heart. And learn but in quietness and stillness to retire to God, and wait upon the Spirit, in whom thou shalt feel peace and joy, in the midst of thy troubles from the cruel and vexatious spirit of the world.

When I open to the flow within me, my perspective widens and deepens. In the waiting, the quality of my emotions and thoughts change; and I too find nourishment.

In this letter, he says, wait to see what God's message is for you. Give yourself space and time to hear.

> Wait to distinguish between God's opening to the words and thine own understanding... always wait for God's season; do not presume to understand a thing before he give thee understanding of it.

In another letter:

> First there is a knowing the will of God; a waiting to know and understand from God what is his holy, good, perfect and acceptable will.

From a letter to M. Hiorns:

Keep cool and low before the Lord, that the seed, the pure living seed, may spring up more and more in thee and thy heart be united more and more to the Lord therein.

Waiting takes us into sacred space. I imagine Penington telling people to be patient, to take their time with Meetings that often continued for several hours. To help them he gives practical advice. *Keep cool and low* is an invitation to bring our attention and breath right down into the abdomen, to become really calm and in touch with the core. Welcome the nourishment of the earth and gather it up into your breath and your heart, so that the seeds within grow and spread within you. *Feel it,* he says over and over again. Feel your heart filled with unconditional love, flowing through you like a fountain. Focus on your heart and imagine it being tended by this love. Wait with openness for what you will be given.

Chapter 4

The Way of the Heart

Trusting our Hearts

Our hearts hold our wisdom; the life that springs up in our hearts is our teacher. Again and again Penington is asking us to listen to our hearts and be guided by love. Love helps us to understand ourselves better, to accept and heal our inner fears with courage and then to forgive ourselves so we can move on. Love is our inner compass that challenges and guides us. The way of love may not always be easy; it may mean being patient with ourselves, opening our hearts to what love asks of us.

Penington says here, let go and listen to the seeds of God's grace deep within, let this spirit fill your heart and guide you:

Give over thine own willing, give over thine own running, give over thine own desiring to know or be anything, and sink down to the seed which God sows in thy heart and let that be in thee and breathe in thee and act in thee.

In a letter to a parent, he writes:

There is a pure principle of life in the heart, from whence all good springs... Mind therefore [God's] leadings in thy heart and wait to be acquainted with its voice there.

Elsewhere he says,

Let the pure, living seed spring up more and more in thee and thy heart be united more and more to the Lord.

This deep wisdom of the universe is within all our hearts and grows in us when we give it space, so that all our actions are shaped by it. Love in our hearts is our guide through life.

There are many traditions where the heart is seen as our centre. In the chakra system, which traces its origins to ancient India, the middle heart chakra is the home of our soul. Just as modern science has revealed the presence and power of energy in the world, so now scientists are recognising that the right brain works with the heart space to empathise, imagine and feel. Way back in the seventeenth century, early Quakers understood this through their own experience. I place my hands across my chest and wait for insights or guidance.

Acceptance and Healing

In the next few passages, I hope to show what Penington taught about the inward journey of listening to the wisdom and love in our hearts, about forgiveness, acceptance and healing. As I read his advice, I sense his great kindness and understanding of the human condition. He asks us to be patient and compassionate towards ourselves, and to let love hold and melt our fears and doubts. As we open ourselves to kindness, we are adding to kindness in the world and are more able to offer it to others.

About forgiveness he says to John Mannock:

when we accept God's mercy and love into our lives... we will have satisfaction in our hearts and hold the truth there.

Asking for forgiveness does not mean we are let off the hook so we can go back to 'wicked ways'. It means acknowledging ourselves as we are and bringing to the light whatever bothers us, our fears, regrets, our bitterness and our anger so we can see them with compassion. Forgiving can then be an act of cleansing that frees us to be more open to love. In a sense part of us is reborn anew.

In another letter to Bridgit Atley he tells her to recognise distressing thoughts, without fear. Don't let them have power over you and they will fall away:

> Wait to feel the relieving measure of life, and heed not distressing thoughts. When they arise ever so strongly in thee… fear them not, but be still awhile, not believing in the power which thou feels they have over thee, and it will fall on a sudden.

This was a time when people worried a lot about good and evil. Penington also wrestled with this, though in a much kinder, softer way than in the dominant Puritan Calvinist-based faith. He tells us to wait in the presence of the spirit, to stop being frightened of the things that worry us. As we accept our anxiety and anger gently with compassion, these will all subside so that we are no longer in their grip. As our burdens feel lifted, we find peace.

To Thomas Walmsley he writes:

> God, who caused the light to shine out of the darkness, out of sin, out of the pollutions of the spirit, into the pure, holy fellowship of living…. Here is unspeakable comfort and satisfaction given by him to the soul, which all the reasonings of men, with all the devices of Satan cannot damp.

Sin, in Penington's terms, means losing the way of the heart. Don't be diverted by your ego, by *temptations and accusations*. Stay with your truth. Live simply, humbly and honestly. Trust in the healing light to flow into the darker areas of our lives, where you will find *unspeakable comfort*.

In this next piece he recognises that this journey may not be easy. Sometimes we will feel vulnerable and broken as he says in this letter:

What tender mother can be more ready to forgive and embrace the child that appears broken and afflicted? Yea, He gives brokenness and He melteth the heart, that he may... embrace it in his arms of reconciliation and in the peace of his spirit.

Accept your vulnerability and be compassionate to yourself.

The Living Christ

For Penington, the way of the heart was more than a route to personal growth and personal peace. The process of letting go of unwanted emotional burdens and habits was all part of the transformation that was necessary in order to step into this new world. The more we can let love work within us, the wiser and kinder we may become. The nearer we come to heaven on earth.

For early Quakers this awakening or opening was like the original Pentecostal experience, in which the power of the living Christ comes to us as a physical and a spiritual reality to transform our lives, in the manner of the early Church. Today most Quakers in Britain avoid this strong image but I think it still needs to be explored. Awakening to Christ's teaching meant being connected to his energy, not simply praying to him or reading about him, but receiving his energy, taking it into ourselves.

In a letter to Thomas Walmsley Penington writes:

if any (one) be truly and really in Christ, he comes to witness a new creation, even the passing of old things, and all things becoming new.

To Friends in Chalfont he writes:

Feed on the tree of life.... O abide in the simplicity that is in Christ, in the naked truth that you have felt there, and there you will be able to distinguish your food, which has several names in Scriptures, which is all the same thing: the bread, the milk, the water.

The 'old' things will pass away as we gradually come to a true understanding of Christ's wisdom. We will see behind shallow rituals that pay lip service to him and discover his true message in our hearts. In the simplicity of stillness, let your *souls and spirits* be nurtured as *we eat and drink* from *the tree of life*. Behind the seventeenth-century Christ-centred faith, I see that Penington is inviting us to embrace this amazing healing spirit and make it fully part of our lives. However we wish to name or interpret it, Penington is calling us to a life of spiritual simplicity, where we are guided and supported by the wisdom of the living spirit within our hearts.

Courage and Wholeness

I have always admired early Quakers' courage and confidence. As they opened themselves to divine love, they experienced an inner power and authority that supported as well as guided them. Penington writes about this in a treatise on Power. This inner power is the life force that starts off as a seed and grows when we give it our loving attention. Trusting in this divine power helps us resolve our own struggles and to face the struggles of the world. He says:

> (true) power is in the little weak stirrings of life in the heart, like a grain of mustard-seed...which springs up as weakness, and leads us on and overcomes our enemies in a mysterious way of working.

As we open our hearts, we will find we have an inner power to bring more and more good things into being. It is a life journey both for oneself and for others, a journey of letting go of the habits and thoughts we don't want and embracing those we do.

Penington's letters are full of encouragement. He writes to Widow Hemmings, don't go to *dead worships* in church, which you know will not lead you to God. Trust that God will look after you as you stand up for your beliefs:

> O what can hurt thee if thy God stand by thee? Take heed of joining with dead worships, which the seed of God in thee disowns... but meekly testify against and abstain from what thou feelest not to be of the Lord.... Is not the Lord stronger than the mountains of prey?

At times like these, when I need courage, I can easily identify with Widow Hemmings. When I feel despairing or frightened, I try to come back to that universal love and wisdom, timeless and everywhere, which we can all turn to for healing.

To these Friends in the Chalfonts, he says your inner power and life will protect you from worldly power and then you will find peace. Keep at it. We will get there.

> For the life and its power is given as a bulwark and weapon against iniquity and its power ... [and when it is overcome] the soul lies down in peace, feeds on the living pastures of life, in peace. You will come to Jerusalem... [where] God and the soul dwell sweetly together... and there is nothing that hath power in it to disturb, annoy or make afraid.

Here I think Penington is referring to both inward and outward struggles to keep faith. He is talking about trusting our inner light to lead us, even when we are challenged by fear, doubts, anger, despair or other demons. Whether these are to do with our personal lives and relationships or our public witness, it is all in the end the same. Trust in the power of love and Light to take care of us.

In a piece that Penington wrote in 1650, he speaks about his own struggles and the need to go ever deeper into understanding, not to give up, but to go deeper and deeper down. This is the path that he is urging us to take. Keep following the way of the heart and more and more will be revealed. On that path we will find the courage, the wisdom and the compassion to live fully and find peace.

Chapter 5

The Meeting as Community

Understanding One Another

Each new Quaker community was an experiment in which Friends aimed to live in accordance with the teachings of the early Church. Each Meeting gave them the support to keep going. In effect, each one was a microcosm of how the world was changing to become heaven on earth. These were exciting times and new Quakers were keen to learn. Penington was one of many leaders who set up and supported new Meetings and his letters are full of advice about how to live well together. Unsurprisingly, he is constantly reminding people to treat each other with the understanding and the love that we give ourselves.

From Aylesbury prison he wrote to Friends in Amersham Meeting:

> Our life is love, and peace, and tenderness; and bearing one with another, and forgiving one another, and not laying accusations against one another; but praying one for another and helping one another up with a tender hand.

> O wait to feel his spirit, and to be guided to walk in this spirit, that you may enjoy the Lord in sweetness, and walk sweetly, meekly, tenderly, peaceably and lovingly one with another.

> So watch your heart and ways; and watch one over another, in that which is gentle and tender.

I can imagine Friends struggling to work together for the good of the whole, so I hope Penington's advice was helpful. His friend

Thomas Ellwood wrote of him that he was a gentle, supportive presence in the Meeting and that he was much missed when he was not there.

Elsewhere Penington reminds us that everyone is important, whoever we are and whatever we do. In a letter to the women's Business Meeting at John Maddock's house, referring to St Paul, he compares the people in the community with parts of the body (1 Corinthians, 12).

[God makes] use of every living member in the living body... every member of the body having life given it, not only for itself [but also] for the use and service of the body. Only dear Friends, [take] great care that every member keep within the limits of life, wherein its capacity and ability of service lies.

He finishes with a reminder to recognise our gifts and to give according to the time and place we find ourselves in. We can never do everything. Being very busy may feel exciting and fulfilling, but sometimes we may need to stand back, to slow down or to do nothing for a while and wait. In the waiting, something valuable may come to us and we find a new direction. It is in giving our gifts that we find our deepest purpose and fulfilment. With our different skills and experiences, we make up the whole. When we work with others, it is rewarding and fun to give space to each person to do what is right for them at that time. In doing that we may find unexpected synergy and creativity.

The Peaceable Kingdom

Sometimes Penington gave advice about difficulties in the Meeting. In this letter we can see how one Friend had taken against another and had refused to go to Meetings at this person's house.

Penington asked him if he had really thought about this person with love:

Is the thing which thou hast against him fully so? Hast thou seen evil in him? Hast thou considered him and dealt with him, as if it had been thy own case? Hast thou pitied him and in tender love laid the thing before him? If thou hast proceeded thus, God's witness in thy conscience will justify thee therein. But if thou hast let in an hardness of spirit or hard reasonings against him, or hard resolution as relating to him, the witness of God will not justify thee in that.

Here he is asking the Friend to consider have you fully understood the person and put yourself in their shoes? 'Have you spoken to them in love?' Or 'have you hardened yourself against them so that you cannot resolve the issue with kindness?'

When I first read this, I was thrilled. Each person needs to fully hear and understand the other, to stand in one another's shoes and see things from the other's perspective. I think this is the first step in conflict resolution of all kinds, however small or large. There must be a certain amount of trust in the process or a willingness to learn and change and an acceptance that we all deserve to be heard and respected. All of this seems to be encapsulated in that short message.

In this next passage Penington demonstrates his own openness and respect towards other people from different churches. The true ground of love and unity, he says, is not in the rules we follow but in meeting one another in the spirit.

Oh how sweet and pleasant it is... to see several sorts of believers, several forms of Christians, everyone learning their own lesson, performing their own peculiar service and knowing, owning and loving one another in their several places... and not quarrelling with one another about their different practices.

For this is the true ground of love and unity, not that such a

man walks and does just as I do, but because I feel the same
Spirit and life in him and that he walks in his own order; and
this is far more pleasing to me than if he walked in just that
track wherein I walk.

How refreshing to read these words at a time when religion
was such an important part of people's lives. While some
worshipped in secret, others switched allegiance depending
on the government's viewpoint. Disputes about salvation and
judgement were deeply entrenched among the Puritans who
hated Catholics and their practices. Puritans saw Catholicism
as demeaning and unpatriotic, full of magical thinking and
mystery, while they on the other hand were part of a brave
new world of reason. I imagine Penington was speaking
mainly about Christians though there were Jews and Muslims
in England at that time. In any case, it is in pieces like this that
we see early Quakers acknowledging a spirit that knows no
cultural or ethnic boundaries.

At the time, the roots of the Quaker Peace Testimony were
being laid. In 1660, George Fox told King Charles II that Quakers
were people of peace. He wrote that Friends *live in that power
and life that takes away the occasion of all wars*. However not all
Friends were ready to be pacifists. Many of them had fought
for Cromwell in the Civil War and many will have been uneasy
at the arrival of the king. To William Penn, Fox said *wear your
sword as long as you can*. There was no police force and people
routinely took the law into their own hands, so *laying down one's
sword* was no easy decision.

Penington recognised that peace was a dream to be worked
towards step by step:

I speak not against any magistrates or peoples, defending
themselves against foreign invasions; or making use of the
sword to suppress the violent and evil-doers within their

borders... but yet there is a better state, which the Lord hath already brought some into and which nations are to expect and travel towards. There is to be a time when *nation shall not lift up sword against nation; neither shall they learn war any more.*

Clearly, he believed that a world without weapons was possible. This was a time when individuals had to protect themselves as best they could. So to even contemplate laying down weapons at that time, would have required amazing trust. I think it is important to recognise the truth of this. People who carry guns or knives today will go on doing so till they feel safe enough to stop. Most of us want to feel safe and to see that there are resources in place to keep things that way. Those who see safety in barriers and armies will not readily give them up in favour of bridges and mediators. It will take persistence, imagination and compassion to create the other way.

Penington's Vision as a Garden

I think this last passage that I have chosen beautifully describes Penington's vision for that peaceful world.

know thy heart more and more ploughed up by the Lord, that his seeds of grace may grow up in thee more and more, and thou mayst daily feel thy heart as a garden, more and more enclosed, watered, dressed and walked in by him.

I see the seeds of grace springing up in our hearts flowering and bearing fruit in the garden nurtured by God's wisdom and love. As each person's heart becomes like a garden, so the whole world will become one wonderful garden. This is not paradise as the Garden of Eden before the Fall nor is it paradise to return to when we die. It is an earthly garden attainable now when our hearts are open to God's grace.

In seventeenth-century England, ordinary gardens were places where people worked together, producing food and herbs, tripping over chickens, hanging out the washing and sitting down to rest when they could. Gardens were organic, living, working places where the people who tended them were at home. It may be that this is an idealised vision but that is all part of the complexity of working towards a vision. For me, the image of the garden says so much about our relationship with ourselves, one another and indeed all of life. A flourishing garden is one where diversity and harmony work together for the good of the whole. Go through the gate, step over the threshold come quietly into the garden with your eyes and ears open and your hands ready to serve. Do what is yours to do, for the wellbeing of the household and the garden.

Penington has talked about listening to the wisdom and compassion in the fountain and the seed, taking this energy into our hearts and working with it to understand ourselves and others, being open to new learning, caring for all of life. The vision of the garden beckons.

Part III
Reflections

Early Quakers saw that personal awakening and social transformation go hand in hand. They had a clear vision of a more equal and compassionate world in which everyone would be guided by the spirit of Christ within. In his writings Penington teaches us what we need to do. The inner work we do will help us to understand ourselves and others so that we have more chance of creating the peaceful, fair and sustainable society we long for. Fortunately for me, Penington's advice is kind and encouraging. The path to understanding can take us deep into tangled woods, as well as to gardens and hilltops.

In this next section on reflections, my starting point is a letter (dated 1670) which I have referred to a few times already.

Wait to know the springings of life... sink very low and become very little; yea know no power to believe, to act or suffer anything for God but as it is given thee by the springing grace, virtue and life of Jesus. For grace is a spiritual, inward thing, an holy seed and is sown by God and springs up in the heart. People have a notion of grace but know not the thing. Do not thou matter the notion, but feel the thing, and know thy heart more and more ploughed up by the Lord, that his seeds of grace may grow up in thee more and more, and thou mayst daily feel thy heart as a garden, more and more enclosed, watered, dressed and walked in by him.

Images, such as the seed and the garden, offer us a gateway into spiritual exploration. They do this by taking us through our senses and imagination beyond words, into our experience. They may call up pictures, sounds, smells or feelings. Or stories and memories. The beauty of Penington's images is that they are mostly about nature, drawing us to the spirit that is flowing and growing within and beyond. Unlike specific devotional objects, I find they can change and move in my imagination.

Reflection 1

The Seed Within

I sit and wait in the stillness. Maybe 'contemplation' is a more useful word than 'worship'. I give myself space to see what happens, trusting that I will receive what I need. Penington invites us to sink low and wait for the seeds of grace to spring up in our hearts. When he says *feel the thing*, he was saying just that; experience it physically and it will infuse your whole life. Give it time. Feel your whole body quieten down and your breath gently soothing every cell, like water from the fountain of life. Wait and listen.

I come into a place that is both still and gently moving. Sometimes it comes easily. I feel the wave of my breath connecting with all the other waves in the ocean of life. I am one with all that is. Sometimes nothing much happens. I remember that my breath is my prayer and deliberately breathe into the centre of my body and being. Then I watch my breath spread out towards the people around me. In the stillness, my thoughts coalesce into new insights from within or beyond. New understanding comes to me, maybe as guidance or as a new perspective. In Meeting for Worship it is easier to come to centre, because I feel held by the people around me and I relax. I am present with the whole of myself, just as I am. I don't know what this practice of opening and listening will reveal. I do know that being centred and held by the group will help me feel safe to explore in this sacred space of mystery. There are many other ways to come into it. Penington's advice to sink low and feel the seeds within is a beautiful beginning.

I think this state of contemplation is what Penington meant by 'grace'. When he writes to us about the seeds of grace, he is saying divine grace is living within us. It is not something to be striven or fought for, because we are each born with it. We simply need to be present and connected to the core of our being and we will find grace waiting for us. Yet the image of the seed shows me that grace is not only a state of being; it is also a state of potential and growth. As we allow ourselves to connect with the seeds of grace springing up in our hearts, we are prompted to make something happen, to create and flourish.

Each seed bursting into life speaks to me of birth and energy and joy. I imagine the seed beginning very small and quiet, deep within and then becoming an upward flowing energy that is like an inner fountain enlivening and awakening us. It is a precious and glorious thing to wait for and connect with. We are blessed to be alive. I remember ministry given by a very old lady to a large group of teenagers about joy being like raspberry jam bubbling up in the pan. I smile at memories of my father testing the jam in the big vat on the cooker. There is something irresistible about joy bubbling up; it is deeper than other emotions because it comes to us from the source of life. When I sink low, I bring my attention to my feet on the earth and breathe deeply, allowing my breath to lift me. I feel upheld by joy.

When we tap into this life-giving energy, I think we can see that, beyond all the struggles and muddles, our world is still precious and wonderful. The Franciscan monk Richard Rohr says joy is revolutionary because it is empowering. It helps turn anger and frustration into a positive energy that draws people in. At times I may be sad or uncertain, yet I know from experience that joy can spill out and help to heal us. It does not dissipate these feelings entirely; they may, however, be less overwhelming, less demanding of our attention, if that is appropriate. Joy is an expansive energy, which helps us to welcome life, so that we feel affirmed and connected to all that is. It draws people to us, because they too feel welcomed and affirmed. The flip side is a contracting energy which comes upon us when we are worried and fearful. Joy can help us see the bigger picture with love, to know what really matters, to laugh at small problems, to recognise the contribution we can make, when and where we can. Joy is the energy of hope. I am thinking of enslaved people who said they kept their sanity by singing. Performing joy feeds us and reminds us that it is good to be alive. Maybe it is time for unprogrammed Meetings to break with tradition and find ways to celebrate. I wonder if our pre-Meeting worship sharing could dare to break into song or dance.

Joy can empower us both personally and politically. As I breathe out and around me, I pray for the world. I ask that more and more people may experience the joy that melts despair, so they are less fearful and more confident to act with compassion and generosity. I feel in touch yet again with the miracle of life and all the healing and awakening around us.

Exercises and Questions

Grace can come to us sometimes spontaneously or sometimes when we ask for it. For me grace is a feeling of wholeness and presence with myself and all that is. I feel connected to the stillness and flow within me and around me.

In his letters Penington often reminds his readers to feel, notice and experience what they find within because that is how we are in touch with our inner flow. For the same reason, the exercises or practices that I am offering here, are all about feeling, noticing and experiencing. They are mainly based on the Alexander Technique and Tai Chi, though of course, there are many similar practices that you may be more familiar with or prefer. This is an invitation for you to explore what works for you.

In the Alexander Technique we talk about non-doing, no effort, softening, noticing and imagining. I think this is important. We are not forcing things to happen; we are opening to possibilities and we are using our imagination and intention to help us. We listen to ourselves. Our breath is the life force that connects us to our core and to all that is. We invite our breath to soften and go where we direct it.

The Practice of Presence

Give yourself about 15 minutes or more to do this exercise. There are many ways to practise presence; this is just one.

- Sit quietly and notice your back and behind against the chair, your feet on the ground, your clothes against your skin. Try to accept any aches and pains with kindness.
- Imagine your breath as a wave, a river or fountain, flowing gently and smoothly through your centre. Let it flow with ease, up from your feet and down from your crown. Notice the flow in the stillness.
- Imagine your eyes softening. Just allow yourself to gaze at what is, noticing without judging, so you are resting and receptive.
- As your eyes and ears soften, do your thoughts slow down and soften? Is there more space between them?
- Can you sense a spaciousness around you?
- Wait and see, until you are ready to finish.
- What have you discovered about yourself?
- What insights or gifts have you received?
- Can you imagine doing this regularly as preparation or rest?

Connecting to Joy

This exercise is about bringing joy into your body; I like to do it in the morning. Do this as slowly as you can comfortably manage, so you can feel and notice what is happening.

- Stand feet slightly apart, hands by your side.
- Bend your knees a little. Start to turn your palms

outwards and upwards.

- As you breathe in, bring your arms out and up in a great arc, on each side, away from your shoulders. Imagine a smile extending across your back and up to your fingertips.
- As you do this, straighten your legs. Let your hands almost meet above your head. Stretch as much as you like.
- Gently breathe out. Bending your knees a little, bring your hands together down your centre in a prayer position.
- Let your hands part and turn your palms down, ready to turn up again to repeat the practice as much as you wish.
- Are you able to do it outside or by a window, so you can connect with nature? If not, can you do this by a plant or a picture?
- How do you feel when you have done it a few times?
- Can you imagine doing it regularly?

At other times we can remember to connect with joy, simply by sitting quietly.

- Sit with both feet on the ground and your hands in your lap.
- Imagine your breath flowing up from the earth and in from the heavens.
- Imagine joy filling every cell in your body.
- Breathe out with joy, love and hope into the space around you.

Reflection 2

Gifts and Community

When I come into Meeting for Worship, I usually look around at the people gathered in the circle and wonder how they are. It is so good to be worshipping with them. Joy reminds us that life is a gift to be appreciated and shared. Each person is special and precious; each of us brings our own contribution to the community. I am distressed by the way human beings have squandered and exploited so much of the planet and so many lives. When we welcome life as a gift, we come into a relationship of gratitude, compassion and sharing. Our whole perspective changes.

The seeds of life within us contain the gifts that were given to us. Each one of us came into this world as a gift for the whole. When we use our gifts, we find our truth and purpose. What are my gifts of the spirit? And what have I been given through my life? I was born with the gifts of my multicultural heritage and the experiences of my parents, that wove themselves into a pattern as I grew and learnt. Gifts are those things that I feel at home with, that I love to do and long to bring into being. Penington reminds us that we each have our own unique gifts and in sharing them we create a rich community. He refers to what Paul says about the gifts of the spirit being faith, hope and love, the greatest of all being love (1 Corinthians,13). Diversity itself is a gift, because as we open ourselves to others, we are supporting one another and discovering new ways of seeing. We are all learning and growing.

Penington teaches us that the spiritual, personal and political threads in our lives all weave together. Offering our gifts with love has the potential to be powerful in ever-widening circles. For several years our Meeting in Henley has had a stall to distribute white poppies for peace a few weeks prior to Remembrance Sunday. For the service the town square fills with the sights and sounds of quasi-military parades and an admiring audience. Most people wear red poppies in memory of the fallen and have not heard of white poppies. In 2021 instead of having a stall we chose a date in October and took white poppies into the market square and simply said to passers-by, 'I would like to give you a white poppy for peace.' We were amazed by the smiles and thanks we received, not knowing whether the recipients understood the meaning of them. In these fleeting relationships, we had reached out to people's common desire for peace. We could only trust that our gift was welcome and that it sowed seeds of understanding.

There are times when we do not recognise our gifts and we need others to show us. In a healthy group or community, we each bring our own gifts for sharing. We appreciate diversity and welcome one another's contributions. Our meeting had a stall in the market square to bring people's attention to COP26, the 2021 UN Conference on Climate Change. We pooled our resources so that between us, we came up with creative ideas for action. We decided to print postcards for people to post in our big green box with messages to the President. We designed and made posters and cards. Then we communicated our plan around the town. On the day, some of us put up the stall. Others invited passers-by to come in and there was always someone to offer them a card and a pen. Each of us contributed our different gifts.

The idea of working with our gifts and sharing them, turns many preconceptions on their heads. It leads to a deep shift in our way of relating to one another, in the family, the community and beyond. It assumes each person has something important to contribute, even when we disagree. At a community meeting about the traffic problems in our neighbourhood, I asked the participants to stop arguing and take time out to listen to one another. I gave them five minutes each to tell us about their worries and wishes. After a few more arguments, this time with me, they agreed to do it. To everyone's surprise, despite their differences, they gradually saw that they all had the same fears and needs. After that, they worked together, using their various skills to form an effective campaigning body. By listening fully to one another, they had started to create a neighbourhood community.

I have a beautiful card given to me by a school in the Philippines, that a group of Quakers used to support. The phrase along the bottom gives thanks for the *circles of compassion in the world*. In Britain today there is a growing awareness of separation and division, even polarisation as we fight for what we believe will help us most. More than ever there is a need for the spirit of community to widen beyond friends and neighbourhoods. From the perspective of gifts and giving we see diversity as an opportunity to enrich our lives and find common purpose. The climate crisis urgently requires that we do this. Instead of exploiting people and planet, the powers that be must support those who are suffering most, by giving direct help to people in need as well as help to install greener technology. All of life is a gift and we all have a part to play.

Exercises and Questions

Discovering Our Gifts

Penington frequently reminds us to know ourselves. Part of the knowing is to know our gifts and how to share them. We may be called to quiet things or to prominent ones, depending on our personality and circumstances. In a workshop I facilitated, I was surprised how few of the participants had thought about their gifts. So I offer this simple exercise, to do with a friend or friends, if possible.

- Sit quietly and recall what you most loved to do as a child. Notice how this feels.
- Follow your memories forward in time. Did you continue to do them or develop them? Did you discover new things you loved to do? Write or draw what you have discovered.
- What do you love doing now? Is there something forgotten from the past that you would like to include now? Keep adding to your work.
- How are you sharing them or how would you like to share them?
- Remember that some things need not be shared in a conspicuous way. Private prayer or writing a journal are options. Our thoughts and prayers are all part of the whole.
- If you are with a partner or in a group, share what you have discovered and invite a response. Maybe they see other gifts that you had not thought of.
- Maybe finish by writing or drawing a reminder of the gifts that mean most to you.

Reflection 3

Rooftop View

Meeting for worship is a time for us to wait, to listen and to pray. It is a place to simply be, and see what happens, to open ourselves to love and wisdom, to receive what we need, whether it is nurture, support, clarity or guidance. There are times when I have a specific question to explore, when I need to push my way through the undergrowth of my thoughts up on to the hilltop for a clearer view. I sit and wait, listening.

If you look at Medieval paintings of the angel telling Mary that she is to give birth to Jesus, you will see that many of them are on a flat Mediterranean rooftop. The angel is a messenger from heaven and has come to her at the highest point in her house. The roof or hilltop is, metaphorically, a place where we are in touch with the divine. I imagine myself up there and wait for my perspective to grow richer and bigger, and lighter, so that I can hold all possibilities. I see my concerns and questions in the round from different people's points of view, different experiences and interpretations. Sometimes I use this practice at home. When my thoughts and emotions are in a great tangle, I draw a house with a flat roof with all the threads spreading out above it. Then I wait in the space I have created around me for further clarity. Or I go for a walk and ask for help.

Negotiation expert William Ury refers to the rooftop metaphor in his book *Getting to Yes with Yourself: And Other Worthy Opponents*. In the meeting about local traffic issues, described earlier, the impact of this perspective was clear; when we had finished our listening session, we had a complete picture so we could step away from our individual positions and see the situation for the whole neighbourhood. To reach that point I had asked them to tell us, 'How is it for you?' 'What do you most care about?' Finally, after all the arguments, each person felt heard.

Sometimes we need to go deeper and ask, 'What are your greatest fears? What are your highest values here? What is in your gift to do?' This becomes an exercise in sitting together in shared stillness, really listening to our calling. I think back to meetings for peace that we held before the Iraq War. We ministered about our pain, our frustration and our anger, and came to see that we did not want to march in the crowd. Our witness needed to express our sadness and solidarity with those who would suffer most. After a time, we decided to organise Meetings for Worship in central London, in the hope that silent gatherings would remind people about the true sadness of war. Since this was before emails were commonplace, it would be no small achievement for our local meeting to draw together Quakers from all over Britain.

Even when we do not find complete agreement, the bigger picture can help us recognise the worth of each one's experience and viewpoint. For a time, Friends in our meeting held worship-sharing meetings with a Jewish group, who wished to understand why Britain Yearly Meeting, the central body of Quakers in Britain, had decided to boycott Israeli Settlement Goods. In the stillness we acknowledged the complexities and differences and came to a place of mutual understanding. Each one of us saw things differently and yet in that special space we were able to acknowledge the grief and fear of most of the Israelis and Palestinians, with its roots in the past.

I had always had a strong sense of shared suffering, because my mother had been a Jewish refugee from Vienna, who was drawn to Quakers for their pacifism and openness. From her, I had gleaned something of the unbearable pain of knowing people wanted to annihilate them. For some Jews that feeling was too harsh to accept and their denial eventually led them to their death. For others, ancestral memory is a constant reminder of utter hatred and cruelty. Yet, the people who demanded their annihilation, were starving in the face of hyperinflation and lack of food. They too were staring at death.

I wish we could stop debating who is suffering most and recognise the universality inherent in all such suffering, so we can learn and move forward together. Can we simply ask one another, 'How is it for you?' The Sufi writer Rumi says 'Out beyond ideas of right doing and wrong doing, is a meadow. I will meet you there'. The web of life connects us all, calling us to understand one another and work together. I think that meeting each other in the meadow is one of the greatest gifts Quakers have to offer. I hope we will always remember that.

Exercises and Questions

Seeing the World Anew

The Ancient Greeks believed that Delphi was the most spirit-filled place on earth, high up above the eucalyptus trees whose leaves gave off a bluish colour from their oil. If you are doing this on your own.

- Imagine yourself in a high place so you are metaphorically nearer the divine.
- Explore a concern you have by drawing and/or writing all the different viewpoints you can think of.
- Do you know people who hold these different views? Spend time thinking about them.
- With a different colour pen, write down what you learn.
- Can you see how these different people might interact with and enrich each other?
- Centre yourself, breathe deeply and gently and wait.
- What do you see now?

Reflection 4

The Wisdom of our Hearts

Penington's letters teach us that our hearts are the place of our wisdom and love. The more we open our hearts, the more we learn about ourselves and others. Our fears, grief, anger and other difficult emotions begin to dissipate. The more we see ourselves, the more we can transform unwanted feelings and open ourselves to unconditional, divine, love. Gradually we see what God is calling us to do. We feel lighter and clearer. In his letters, Penington recognises that this is not an easy path. His advice is to notice and accept ourselves as we are, to wait and let divine love transform our difficulties. Just keep opening our hearts to them. I put my hands on my heart and wait and listen. For now, my inner conflicts are gradually reconciled and I am more at peace. Each time I learn something new. It is a process of awakening that is important for the whole world, as well as for ourselves individually.

When we are guided more by that still voice in our hearts, we are led less by our fears and anger. In this practice, I have come to see that most human beings on some level know just how precarious our existence is. We respond in the usual animal ways of either fight, flight or freeze. Some of us are doing our best to forge a new way, while others resist change or deny that it is necessary. Others cannot cope with it at all. When I am out on the street campaigning, I try to reach people with kindness, wherever they are and to speak to them from that place of common humanity and fear.

Richard Rohr says that if we do not transform our fears, we will surely transmit them. I think there is a growing understanding of collective trauma in which fear and anger are passed down through the generations, whether from enslavement, racial harassment, the cruelty of war, domestic abuse or other causes. There is evidence that these patterns of suffering become embedded in our DNA and without realising it, we can get caught up in the repeating pattern of fear, resentment and anger. Often this shows itself in a continuing cycle of violence where revenge and fury play out over and over again. Or it leaks out in unexpressed emotions. My mother refused to share her experiences of being Jewish in Vienna during the 1930s, so that her pain hung in the air at home, unspoken and unresolved. Unable to hug or even touch people outside her family, all she said was that she would never allow herself to cry, lest she couldn't stop. Over her life she channelled her experiences into work she did towards peace and international understanding. Yet the layers of ancestral struggle were deep. I know how little she trusted others and what it cost her to keep going.

I know that for my own peace of mind and for the future of the world, we humans need to learn about this. When we look through the eyes of fear or jealousy or cruelty there will be more violence in homes, on the streets and in wars. When we look through the eyes of love, sharing and kindness, we have an opportunity to create a kinder, fairer and more united world. Some people believe that by dying on the cross Jesus calls us to stop the cycle of violence through forgiveness. I am reminded of huge outdoor murals that I saw in Nicaragua, each depicting a crucified leader. At that time liberation theology was an intrinsic part of their struggle for democracy and I wondered about the meaning of those images. I hope they were calling people to keep faith with the Christian message of peace, to stop the cycle of revenge and build relationships with compassion. Every faith calls us to do this; I hope we are all starting to listen more.

Exercises and Questions

As we listen to the wisdom of our heart we are healing ourselves and the world. For ourselves this is an act of cleansing so that we are more able to hear our inner truth and our inner calling. For the world it is an act of peace-making on a deep level of healing.

The Heart Space

Some people find this is a very moving experience so please be gentle with yourself. Read the instructions through to see whether you think this will work for you. It helps to feel yourself held by love, so you may wish to imagine yourself in a safe, kind place, perhaps imagine yourself hugged by someone you love, in the present or from the past. Do this either sitting or lying down. Allow 15 minutes or more.

- Put your hands on your chest if you are comfortable with this and invite your heart space to open.
- Imagine yourself held by love or by a loving presence. Feel the warmth and support of that love. You may wish to stroke your arms and hands.
- If negative feelings come to the surface, invite love to soften them. Place your hands on your heart.
- Imagine your heart space becoming an ocean of love. Acknowledge any difficult feelings and see whether they may be soothed by love. Notice any change that may have occurred.
- Breathe out what you no longer need to hold on to. Breathe in the resources you do need such as love, courage, humour and hope.
- Do this for a while, no effort, just imagine and trust.
- How was that for you?
- What did you learn? What if anything, has changed for you?
- Come out of this exercise slowly and gently.

Reflection 5

The Way of Peace

Inner and outer peace go hand in hand. As we allow the spirit to reveal itself in our hearts, we are taking a journey in compassion and understanding for ourselves and for others. Penington says it all. He speaks directly to us today.

During lockdown in the spring of 2020, I took a photo of the rooftops and the satellite dish from my bedroom window. It seemed to epitomise the way connections to the world had shrunk to a digital shadow of reality. I see community as ever-widening circles of compassion from family and friends to neighbourhoods and out beyond forever. Yet there we were trapped in our *halls of mirrors*, only seeing and hearing the views and experiences that are like ours. I tried to turn the mirrors into windows so I could at least look out and see something different. One of the big lessons of the Covid pandemic is that community must be more than our immediate circle; it must stretch out to embrace the whole world. Otherwise, we are unlikely to survive.

In 2020, Henley Quakers decided to ask permission to lay a white poppy wreath for peace at the Remembrance Service outside the Town Hall along with the red poppy wreaths. On these occasions most people look reassured, while I feel the opposite, frightened by symbols of violence. To offer a white wreath could be seen as a challenge. Yet when I stand back and look at the bigger picture, I see that most of us need to feel safe; we just have different ways of feeling and thinking about safety. Safety is a fundamental need. When we offer a white poppy, we acknowledge this. We say we recognise and honour the pain and suffering which is at the core of remembrance. We understand you. Please understand that for us, promoting peace is part of our honouring. It is possible, both to remember the suffering and to work towards a world where that suffering will not occur. We felt it was time to reach out and ask for our message to be included.

Permission to lay our wreath was granted and now I wonder why I ever feared that it would be refused. Perhaps they were pleased we were joining them. Had we assumed the worst and failed to see they wanted us to stand with them? I don't know. What I do know is that we are called to connect with the best in one another and wherever possible to come alongside one another.

In peace-making, listening with respect and compassion is essential. People need the space to be heard and to hear themselves. As we move towards mutual understanding, we see things from multiple perspectives with empathy and compassion. We see the wider context and how the social and economic structures work for some and against others. Much of Quaker work today embodies this premise of listening. Quiet diplomacy, conciliation, peace education and nonviolence training all incorporate these principles. These, I think, are some of the most powerful ways to heal the world.

Exercises and Questions

Listening is the key to the Quaker way, listening not just when there is a conflict but as a door to deeper mutual understanding. This means listening to our inner selves and speaking the truths we discover in the listening. It is not saying one person is right and the other wrong, or that one person's truth is more valid. It is saying all of us have experience and wisdom to share. We all have a right to be heard.

Behind the Words

Do this in pairs if possible (otherwise use your imagination).

- Each face the other with clenched fists and hold this position for a couple of minutes. Notice what that feels like.
- Shake your hands out, away from each other.
- Now face each other with soft open palms for a couple more minutes Notice what that feels like. Is it different or not?
- In turn, describe what the two positions felt like. Listen without comment.
- What does this tell us about conflict and emotions?

Another way to get behind the words is to do a role play or mime (either with others or on your own).

- Choose a person you wish to understand better.
- Think about the way they behave, move, speak, look.
- Imitate them as best you can. Try to step into their shoes.
- If you are in a pair or group, have someone interview you in that role.
- Debrief yourself. How did you feel? What have you learnt about yourself and the other person?
- What can you do with this learning?

One thing I know is that we are all human beings with our own life stories and the right to express our experiences and beliefs. Most people spend their lives doing the best they can in the circumstances. Mutual understanding leads us to recognise each other, fully for who we are and what we did. Many of us have done the most wonderful and courageous things in terrible situations and somehow the human spirit has flourished. Some of us have done cruel things. Understanding and forgiveness help us to move on together.

Reflection 6

The Garden

I sit with the image of the seed as the source of life, bearing flowers and fruit. To feel our hearts as a garden is to make our lives a garden, in which we all flourish. For me, the garden stands as a metaphor for my vision for the world, spiritually, socially and ecologically. It tells us about our relationships with ourselves, with others and with all of life on the planet. It is also a metaphor for hope that in the end we will save the planet and ourselves, as a species. Penington's image of the seventeenth-century working garden points the way.

In many cultures the garden is a symbol of paradise where God brings us balm. The symbols of nature that are woven into Muslim prayer rugs help people to connect to the nurturing power of all that is green, whether they are in the desert or the city. In the Bible, the Garden of Eden is the original paradise where Adam and Eve ate the forbidden fruit and discovered the difference between good and evil. It was the place where they woke up and learnt about the frailty and potential of being human. The garden is a place of both spiritual and physical nourishment and also of growth and learning.

What does the garden teach about our relationship with people and the planet now? Look beneath the surface and the garden is the beautiful, living, changing world. I am fortunate to have a town garden with trees and a pond as well as flower beds and grass. When we first moved here, I was worried that ground elder would overtake everything, and that precious half hidden gems like lilies of the valley would disappear because of my neglect. Then I came to see that the garden has a life of its own. We are always surprised by what appears as well as what dies away. Every year we marvel at the first snowdrop under the pear tree and the tadpoles teeming in the pond. Humans are not here to dominate. My original instinct to control has given way to watching and waiting, giving a little help to the different plants and animals to flourish in harmony. I could give it over to complete wilding but I won't do that. I belong in the garden too, and my role is to live in it wisely.

I sit by the pond and think about our planet. In the name of progress, we have done some wonderful things and made some terrible mistakes. Fortunately, we can see what we have done, and we still have the capacity to turn ourselves around. I think about people who work with the soil, such as small-scale farmers in Africa finding innovative ways to adapt to climate change. Outside Henley, there is a small cattle farm devoted to regenerative farming, learning from nature, allowing the soil to be restored and biodiversity to return. Elsewhere beavers are being allowed back into the UK to help slow down the flow of rivers so that flooding is less serious. In China the Loess Plateau is becoming productive again after years of over farming that turned it into a desert. Can we re-envisage ourselves as healing gardeners?

The garden demonstrates the value of diversity and co-creation both socially as well as ecologically. Just as a garden needs biodiversity, so a caring society needs to welcome human diversity. In a vibrant and diverse society we acknowledge both our similarities and our differences, we rejoice in them and forgive one another for our misunderstandings. We talk and listen, respect and understand, share and co-operate. We share our gifts of experience and knowledge so that we learn and work together for common purposes. I wonder whether the ideal of equality is a mirage, which you think you see but when you arrive, it is somewhere else. Diversity does not demand absolute equality; it does require mutual understanding, resources for all, space to be who we are, exchange of ideas, fears and hopes. I wonder about forgiveness in this process. I am thinking about the work of two South Africans, a black ANC General and a white woman whose daughter was killed in one of the attacks he planned. Their journey is the subject of the film *Beyond Forgiving* by Initiatives of Change. Having forgiven one another, these two people have helped communities all over the world to find healing after conflict. In the film, the people in the workshops recognise each other's humanity and vulnerability. They celebrate what they have learnt about each other and move forward together.

As a metaphor of hope, the garden reminds us that through history, people have longed to recreate the world as a place of peace, harmony, diversity, nurture, productivity, fertility and community. Early Quakers like Penington, had a deep belief that society could be transformed through the working of the spirit in our hearts. So strong was that belief, that they expected it to happen soon. The path of awakening is a joyful one. At times it may be hard. It requires attention to the spirit, to our particular gifts and insights, to our leadings and discoveries. It calls us to use our gifts in different ways, so we can contribute to the whole and find our own wholeness. All these things are available to us in the metaphor of the seeds of grace springing up in our hearts to become a garden walked in and watered by God.

Exercises and Questions

Today we too need beliefs and a vision that will help us cherish all of life and transform the world. As we look to the future it is difficult to have the confidence of the early Quakers. Yet hope can still spring eternal in our hearts. There is a transcendent quality about hope, which like love and joy, it pours into our hearts when we open ourselves to it. It may seem like a tiny glimmer at the far end of a tunnel, yet it can move mountains.

Here are some ideas that might give you hope:

Hope as Practice

Noticing the good things:

- Look out for examples of good things happening.
- Support them with prayer or funding or telling others about them.
- Keep a note of them as a reminder to yourself.
- If you have the time and energy, get involved actively.

Working with Your Vision

- Start by thinking about the qualities and values that are important to you.
- Get them down on paper, as a list or a piece of writing, a drawing or diagram.
- Maybe keep it for a while and add to it later.
- How do these qualities and values translate into your vision and hopes?
- What does your vision look like? Imagine yourself in that place.
- What might you be doing more of such as talking to strangers, walking or cycling, shopping locally and sustainably, joining a community project.
- Commit to some of these activities and see how you feel.
- Maybe go a step further and find campaigns that support your vision. Collect information about them.

Experimental Prayer

- Sit quietly, put your hands on your chest and open your heart space.
- Connect to your breath, flowing in and out.
- Say to yourself: *Hope, love and joy are springing up in my heart as I breathe in the peace and presence of the divine.*
- Stay with this as long as you wish. Hope, love and joy are all gifts of the spirit.

Finally

The Seed and the Garden

I stop to listen to the silence and feel it touching me. Silence connects me to the beginning of the universe when life was created from the seed. I sit quietly and remember who I am, created from the elements, from time and space, from silence. Planets, plants, people and projects are all part of the continuing cycle of life that starts with the seed within and flows out into fruition. Keep listening and learning. Don't make assumptions. Find the truth in the other's experience. Open you heart to new possibilities. The seed in each person is full of potential, containing our truth and our gifts. From a state of waiting and being, we follow our inner promptings with love and integrity, offering our gifts to the world for sharing. Our inner knowing guides our outward actions. Stillness gives way to movement. Each action is an act of creation. Our hearts open as we welcome new connections. The more we listen and respond, the more we learn about ourselves and others, the more wisdom we gather. As we follow the promptings of our hearts and the calling of our gifts, the seed will flower and contribute to the creation of the garden in our lives and in the world. Living from our still centre, we act with integrity and authority, as well as with compassion and wisdom. I sit with the image of the garden that is walked in and watered by the universal spirit in all of us.

It is in a vision such as this, where my hope for our future lies. The early Quakers responded to the chaos around them by challenging the status quo from within. This was a radical way of being that offers us deep wisdom in the melting pot of all our current problems. Today I pray that more and more people will discover the truths in this teaching, as we seek to save ourselves and create a kinder, fairer world.

Bibliography

Leach, Robert J (ed.). *The Inward Journey of Isaac Penington: an abbreviation of Penington's works.* Wallingford, Pa: 1945 (Pendle Hill Pamphlets, 29)

Penington, Isaac, *The Works of Isaac Penington,* online: http://www.qhpress.org/texts/penington/. Quaker Heritage Press, 1995–97

Penington, Mary. *On Quakers, medicine and property: the autobiography of Mary Penington (1624–1682).* Cambridge, Mass.: Rhwymbooks, 2000

Quaker faith and practice: the book of Christian discipline of the Yearly Meeting of the Religious Society of Friends (Quakers) in Britain. 5th revised edition. London: Britain Yearly Meeting, 2013

Snell, Beatrice Saxon. *A month with Isaac Penington.* London: Quaker Home Service, 1966

THE NEW OPEN SPACES

Throughout the two thousand years of Christian tradition there
have been, and still are, groups and individuals that exist in
the margins and upon the edge of faith. But in Christianity's
contrapuntal history it has often been these outcasts and
pioneers that have forged contemporary orthodoxy out
of former radicalism as belief evolves to engage with and
encompass the ever-changing social and scientific realities. Real
faith lies not in the comfortable certainties of the Orthodox,
but somewhere in a half-glimpsed hinterland on the dirt track
to Emmaus, where the Death of God meets the Resurrection,
where the supernatural Christ meets the historical Jesus,
and where the revolution liberates both the oppressed and
the oppressors.

Welcome to Christian Alternative... a space at the edge where
the light shines through.

If you have enjoyed this book, why not tell other readers by
posting a review on your preferred book site.

Recent bestsellers from Christian Alternative are:

Bread Not Stones
The Autobiography of An Eventful Life
Una Kroll
The spiritual autobiography of a truly remarkable woman
and a history of the struggle for ordination in the Church of
England.
Paperback: 978-1-78279-804-0 ebook: 978-1-78279-805-7

The Quaker Way
A Rediscovery
Rex Ambler
Although fairly well known, Quakerism is not well understood.
The purpose of this book is to explain how Quakerism works as
a spiritual practice.
Paperback: 978-1-78099-657-8 ebook: 978-1-78099-658-5

Blue Sky God
The Evolution of Science and Christianity
Don MacGregor
Quantum consciousness, morphic fields and blue-sky
thinking about God and Jesus the Christ.
Paperback: 978-1-84694-937-1 ebook: 978-1-84694-938-8

Celtic Wheel of the Year
Tess Ward
An original and inspiring selection of prayers combining
Christian and Celtic Pagan traditions, and interweaving their
calendars into a single pattern of prayer for every morning
and night of the year.
Paperback: 978-1-90504-795-6

Christian Atheist
Belonging without Believing
Brian Mountford
Christian Atheists don't believe in God but miss him: especially the transcendent beauty of his music, language, ethics, and community.
Paperback: 978-1-84694-439-0 ebook: 978-1-84694-929-6

Compassion Or Apocalypse?
A Comprehensible Guide to the Thoughts of René Girard
James Warren
How René Girard changes the way we think about God and the Bible, and its relevance for our apocalypse-threatened world.
Paperback: 978-1-78279-073-0 ebook: 978-1-78279-072-3

Diary Of A Gay Priest
The Tightrope Walker
Rev. Dr. Malcolm Johnson
Full of anecdotes and amusing stories, but the Church is still a dangerous place for a gay priest.
Paperback: 978-1-78279-002-0 ebook: 978-1-78099-999-9

Do You Need God?
Exploring Different Paths to Spirituality Even For Atheists
Rory J.Q. Barnes
An unbiased guide to the building blocks of spiritual belief.
Paperback: 978-1-78279-380-9 ebook: 978-1-78279-379-3

Readers of ebooks can buy or view any of these bestsellers by clicking on the live link in the title. Most titles are published in paperback and as an ebook. Paperbacks are available in traditional bookshops. Both print and ebook formats are available online.

Find more titles and sign up to our readers' newsletter at
http://www.johnhuntpublishing.com/christianity
Follow us on Facebook at
https://www.facebook.com/ChristianAlternative

We hope you enjoyed this Hay House book. If you'd like to receive our online catalog featuring additional information on Hay House books and products, or if you'd like to find out more about the Hay Foundation, please contact:

Hay House, Inc., P.O. Box 5100, Carlsbad, CA 92018-5100
(760) 431-7695 or (800) 654-5126
(760) 431-6948 (fax) or (800) 650-5115 (fax)
www.hayhouse.com® • www.hayfoundation.org

———

Published in Australia by: Hay House Australia Pty. Ltd.,
18/36 Ralph St., Alexandria NSW 2015
Phone: 612-9669-4299 • *Fax:* 612-9669-4144
www.hayhouse.com.au

Published in the United Kingdom by: Hay House UK, Ltd.,
The Sixth Floor, Watson House, 54 Baker Street, London W1U 7BU
Phone: +44 (0)20 3927 7290 • *Fax:* +44 (0)20 3927 7291
www.hayhouse.co.uk

Published in India by: Hay House Publishers India,
Muskaan Complex, Plot No. 3, B-2, Vasant Kunj, New Delhi 110 070
Phone: 91-11-4176-1620 • *Fax:* 91-11-4176-1630
www.hayhouse.co.in

———

Access New Knowledge.
Anytime. Anywhere.

Learn and evolve at your own pace
with the world's leading experts.

www.hayhouseU.com